MARRIAGE
GOD CREATED IT
I'm Loving It

MARRIAGE
GOD CREATED IT
I'm Loving It

Lavetta Wilson McClam

Copyright © 2018 by Lavetta Wilson McClam

All Scripture quotations in this book are taken from the King James Version of the Bible, unless otherwise noted in the text. Scriptures marked AMP are taken from the Amplified Bible. Scriptures marked NIV are taken from the New International Version of the Bible.

The author has chosen to capitalize specific words relating to the Lord and His Kingdom and any pronouns referring to the Deity. The author also has chosen to not capitalize the name of satan or any names relating to his kingdom; e.g.; devil and (the) enemy.

All rights reserved under International Copyright Law. No part of this book may be reproduced, stored in a retrieval system, or transmitted in any form or by any means without prior written permission of the author, except for the inclusion of brief quotations in printed reviews.

ISBN 978-0-9990646-0-3

For information about this book or to contact the author, write to: mcclam221@gmail.com

Published by: Lavetta Wilson McClam

Published in the United States of America.

Dedication

I would like to dedicate this book to my parents, John and Annie Mae Wilson—two people who gave of themselves and expected nothing in return. They taught me values that molded and shaped my life. I'll never forget this statement that they often made to my siblings and me:

"Put God first, work hard, don't lie, cheat, or steal, and you will be successful—not man's measurements of success, but God's."

My father, John Charles Wilson, who was very much alive when I started writing and had become a motivational speaker, is no longer with us. He died December 7, 2010. My ability to write this book came from my father, not because he was a scholar or a profound author, but because he wasn't fearful. He taught and shared things with me that encouraged and motivated me to not be afraid of the unknown. His words of wisdom are written on the tablet of my heart.

My mother, Anne Mae Graham Wilson, is a prayer warrior and the most consistent person I know. She always said, the truth will stand forever and a lie will fall. In my forty-six years of living, being consistent in my life, my values, and my beliefs has revealed the truth of who I am. Now when I write and stand before people, who I am has already been revealed. Mom, I thank you for praying for me in and out of season and being a mother who listened with her heart. From the time of my childhood to the woman that I am now, you have always been the same.

What a blessing to have great parents!

Acknowledgments

To my husband, Wayne Bethea McClam. This book would have never existed without you. You have heard every word that is written in this book a million times, and you have never tried to change my opinion or my thoughts. You have encouraged me to do things that I never thought I could do, such as write a book. God used you to pull the best out of me. You have truly laid down your life for me. What a blessing to have a husband like you.

I love you, Wayne.

To my sons, Dewayne and Jarvis, I thank God for you. He has entrusted me to be a steward over you. In return, both of you have taught me how to be a mother. I can barely remember you as babies, because you both grew up so fast. Put God first in all that you do, and in all things give Him thanks. I am so proud of you both. What a blessing to have sons like the two of you.

Love, Momma

Marriage

To my siblings, Terry, Don, Sharon, Angela, Shawn, and Marilyn. What a wonderful life we had growing up together. Never a dull moment. I called each of you by name because, in your own special way, you have blessed me like no other. What a blessing to have siblings like you.

    I love you guys.

My sister in Christ, Jennifer: I thank you for taking the time to share your knowledge and input to make this possible. You were never too busy to answer my questions or give me your advice on certain matters. What a blessing to have a person like you in my life.

    You're the best.

Contents

Foreword 1
Introduction 3
Willpower 13
Killing Me Softly 19
Harsh Words 23
Something is Missing 27
I Am an Individual 31
Whose Money Is It? 35
Why Do I Seem to Love Him More? 43
No Ordinary Love 47
The Vows Make the Difference 51
Forgive Quickly 57
Your Spouse Must Be First 63
Respect Always 67
Don't Forget the Sex 71
Prayer Changes Things 75
Notes 79
Final Thoughts 83
A Prayer for You 85
About the Author 87

Foreword

I met her at a carwash and she was as lovely as she is now. Actually, her car said "Lovely Lavetta" on the front tag. As I got to know her, I found out that this was the person I wanted to marry. Then it happened; a year and half later, we got married, and I can actually say that I love being married. I am loving it because I thought all it took to have a happy marriage was to say I do, have children, go to work, pay bills, and have sex. Boy, was I in for a surprise!

The author of this book, Lavetta McClam—my wife of twenty-five years—and I have experienced together the highs, lows, and the in-betweens. She is a woman of God who does not compromise the Word of God for anything or anyone. The things she shares in this book are based from experience. I supported this book from day one and never told her what to write.

Being married to Lavetta has been the best thing to ever happen to me. She was my wife for sixteen of the twenty-one years I served in the Marine Corps, and she supported every deployment, duty, and war.

I hope this book encourages you, the reader, to fight the good fight of Faith and not let the devil destroy your marriage. If you are not married, this book will give you insight about how satan uses everything and anything or anyone to destroy what God has ordained. I truly believe that life experiences are the best teachers. Lavetta became transparent in this book so that others, too, can have the joy and happiness in their marriage that God wants for them. I thank God that she was obedient to His direction.

Lavetta, I love being married to you.

Wayne B. McClam
"All it takes is all you got."

Introduction

So many people ask me whether I am truly happily married. And if marriage is such a good thing, why is the divorce rate so high? They wonder how the person they committed to spending the rest of their life with—in sickness and in health, for richer and for poorer—wound up as their enemy. They also wonder why they no longer enjoy the very things they both used to love.

At the beginning of relationships, most couples confess a shared goal of being together forever. But before being married even a year, many are headed for trouble and unsure of what to do.

The issues that arise can be deep or shallow. I remember a time when my husband Wayne and I couldn't agree on how to fold bath towels! We stood in front of God, friends, and family committing to spend the rest of our lives together, yet we couldn't agree on how to fold a towel. We both felt that since we were taught how to fold by our mothers, surely neither one of them could be wrong. Amazingly, it ended up taking three years to work toward a compromise.

Marriage

In thinking back on that time, we now realize that it didn't matter how the towels were folded. Each of our parents had taught us well—and in their own special way. The lesson for us was to understand the differences in communication and expression, and to learn that doing things differently shouldn't be considered wrong. I can truly say that I love being married, and I have been sharing this message with others for the past twenty years, although I've been married for more than twenty-five years.

During the first five years of our marriage, I knew that I loved my husband, but I didn't necessarily love being married. I didn't think much about the commitment marriage required until after I said, "I do." Sure, we had a very nice wedding, and Wayne and I repeated everything the minister instructed us to say. But in the middle of the reception, I said to myself, "What did I just do?" Then I answered myself and said, "Girl, you just got *married* and *promised* to be with this man for the rest of your life."

But I didn't stop there. I continued talking to myself until I came up with a Plan B—specifically, that if this marriage thing doesn't work, I'd just get a *divorce*. Can you believe this was at our wedding reception? What a way to start a marriage! Wayne had no idea that, from the very beginning, I had a Plan B that didn't include him.

From that first day, I learned that a marriage will not work on its own. You have to work it, and I found out how. Twenty-five years later, I'm still married, I no

Introduction

longer have a Plan B, and I love the freedom I have in loving my spouse!

Wayne and I share a long history. We met in junior high school when my cousin took me to a skating rink in a small town in South Carolina. Wayne was there skating, and from what I could tell, he appeared to be good at it. I figured he must have spent a lot of time at the rink. I skated pretty well myself, but I'd developed the skill after falling again and again on the hard cement of my parents' driveway.

That night, we talked and he kissed me—yes, my first kiss. I wrote him a letter the following week, but he didn't respond. I felt rejected; a first kiss with no response can leave a girl feeling pretty bad about herself. Because we lived in the same small town, I would see him on occasion, but we didn't talk again for seven years. By that time, we had both graduated from high school and he had entered the United States Marine Corps.

It was interesting that, when we had met years earlier, he was still a young teenage boy— but after seven years, it was clear that he was a well-traveled young man with more life experiences. I was a confident young lady, and you would have thought that I, too, had traveled around the world. However, I was a college dropout, living with my parents and waiting on the next semester to start.

During this interim period of my life, I had made plans to move into my own apartment, so I wasn't interested in playing games. I had been there and done that. I was ready to be the person God had created me to be. I didn't have a clue about how to be this person, but I knew that I had to do something different. So I began to focus on positive things and my family, since they were the people who loved me no matter what.

I'll never forget that day Wayne and I met for the second time. I had just spent the day hanging out with my parents at Myrtle Beach, South Carolina, and sand from the beach coated the interior of my car. I took my parents home and decided I would go to the car wash to vacuum it out. I was there no more than five minutes when a car with a couple of young men passed by. They noticed me, turned around, and came back to where I was cleaning my car, but I acted as if I didn't see them. Wayne got out of the car, and his friend drove away. The first thing he said to me was, "Let me do that for you." It was as if that rejection from junior high school never happened.

From then on, we then started going places together and became good friends; we laughed and talked a lot. That fall, as planned, I moved into my own apartment, and Wayne and I began to date. Our lives changed forever. A year later, we were married.

Not everyone will get married, but for those of us who choose to, marriage is more than saying, "I do." I have always been a good lover and friend to Wayne, but I wasn't always a good wife—not because I didn't want to be, but simply

Introduction

because I didn't know how to be. I have read and heard people say that couples date and get married for three reasons: physical attraction, soulish attraction, and spiritual attraction. I agree; however, I believe that most couples are divorced before they get to the spiritual attraction. We get so caught up in the physical and soulish attraction that we never connect spiritually, even though that is the most important element of marriage.

We must understand that the nature of man has three parts: Man is a spirit; we live in a body; and we have a soul:

"And the very God of peace sanctify you wholly; and I pray God your whole spirit and soul and body be preserved blameless unto the coming of our Lord Jesus Christ."

1 THESSALONIANS 5:23

If you are not living a godly life—or you have not accepted Jesus Christ as your Lord and Savior—your spirit is dead toward the things of God and your soul and body are in control. Man became spiritually dead when Adam ate from the tree of knowledge of good and evil:

> *"But of the tree of the knowledge of good and evil you shall not eat, for in the day that you eat of it you shall surely die."*
>
> GENESIS 2:17

Because of Adam's sin, spiritual death infected the human race. That is why Jesus told Nicodemus that a man must be *born again*. Just like so many of us, Nicodemus did not have a clue as to what Jesus was talking about.

When Wayne and I got married, we were both spiritually dead. We did not have a relationship with God, so we made decisions based on physical attraction (performance and appearance) and soulish attractions (will and emotions)—and you know, these things are ever-changing. What I've learned during the tenure of twenty-five years of marriage is that spiritual attraction helps hold the physical and soulish attraction in true perspective. Spiritual attraction helps us to think beyond ourselves and gives us the desire to do what is pleasing to God, who is the Creator of marriage. When we build upon our spiritual attraction, our physical and soulish attraction intensifies:

Introduction

"*Verily, verily, I say unto thee, except a man be born again, he cannot see the kingdom of God.*"

JOHN 3:1–7

Marriage is an institution designed and ordained by God. We have certain commitments, obligations, and duties that are symbolic. The roles that God has given to Wayne and I are intended to symbolize and represent a greater reality. While marriage is temporal—(even though I really want to be married to Wayne in heaven, I came to the realization that it wouldn't be fair to all the women who were never married)—the reality that marriage symbolizes is eternal.

The reality that explains the attitudes and conduct of our marriage is the relationship of Jesus Christ to His church. (Jesus laid down His life for the church.) Like many other married couples, we did not understand this relationship clearly. "It was a great mystery:"

Marriage

For we are members of His body, of His flesh, and of His bones. For this cause shall a man leave his father and mother, and shall be joined unto his wife, and they two shall be one flesh. This is a great mystery: but I speak concerning Christ and the church.

EPHESIANS 5:30-32

This mystery is clear to me now, and my conduct in marriage is to be a reflection of this mystery that I now understand.

When I began to understand the relationship between Christ and the church, I started to enjoy my role as a wife. I would be lying if I said it happened overnight, because it didn't. My way of thinking had to change. First, I made the decision to live a godly life and no longer be conformed by society, but to be transformed by the renewing of my mind, so I would know what is good, what is acceptable, and what is the perfect will of God for my life/marriage:

Introduction

Do not be conformed to this world (this age), [fashioned after and adapted to its external, superficial customs], but be transformed (changed) by the [entire] renewal of your mind [by its new ideals and its new attitude], so that you may prove [for yourselves] what is the good and acceptable and perfect will of God, even the thing which is good and acceptable and perfect [in His sight for you].

ROMANS 12:2, AMP

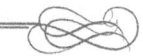

Instead of being molded by the values of this world, I allowed myself to be transformed; that is, changed by the renewing of my mind. A good marriage transformation starts in the mind and heart. A marriage dedicated to the world and its concerns is a marriage that will be tossed back and forth by the current of life. But a mind dedicated to God's truth will produce a marriage that will truly last until "death do us part."

In this book, I will share with you those things that God imparted to me that undoubtedly saved my marriage.

Willpower

The proverbs of Solomon, the son of David, king of Israel; to know wisdom and instruction; to perceive the words of understanding; to receive the instruction of wisdom, justice, and judgment, and equity; to give subtilty to the simple, to the young man knowledge and discretion. A wise man will hear, and will increase learning; and a man of understanding shall attain unto wise counsels: to understand a proverb, and the interpretation; the words of the wise, and their dark sayings. The fear of the LORD is the beginning of knowledge: but fools despise wisdom and instruction.

PROVERBS 1:1-7

Willpower is a very familiar word, but what is it really, and where does it come from? I don't know much about the word willpower, but I am sure that my mother has it, because she and my father were married for more than forty years. My grandmother must have it as well— based on the stories she told us about our grandfather—and they were married for fifty-plus years. My mother-in-law must have it too, because no matter what, she is not moved by what my father-in-law does.

So what in the world is wrong with me? I can remember the day that God told me I needed to rely on and trust Him in my marriage. He said, "You can read all the books in the world, listen to all the compact discs ever recorded, or go to every marriage seminar, but you will still be unhappy if you don't know My will for your marriage."

God prepared a helpmate for Adam and they stayed together. Yes, Adam and Eve were married for years. God assured me that the problems we are having today in our marriages are not unique. Eve opened the door for satan, which caused her and Adam to be kicked out of their home (the Garden of Eden).

But Adam still understood that Eve was created to help him; therefore, he did not hold a grudge against her. Together, they learned from their mistakes and continued on as husband and wife. Adam knew that there was no other woman made for him.

Wayne and I made the decision to get married, and what we need now is the *Willpower* to remain married.

> **Willpower** is the ability and strength of mind to carry out one's decisions, wishes, or plans.

- **Ability** is the physical, mental, and spiritual power to perform.

- **Strength** is the power to withstand strain, force, and stress.

So it is safe to say that willpower is the physical, mental, and spiritual power to perform and withstand strain, force, and stress, in order to carry out one's decisions, wishes, and plans.

For five years, I did it my way, and I got my results. But my way did not give me ability or strength. I was physically and mentally drained, so I didn't have the power to withstand the strain, the force, or the stress that came with being a wife. Instead, I relied on what I knew best: my personality. I was used to getting what I wanted. Nagging a person— continually complaining or faultfinding—until they gave in was normal for me.

It's funny because, over the years, I didn't see it as nagging; I saw it as being *persistent*. For many years I worked in sales, and I always was a top salesperson. So in the beginning of our marriage, I spent most of my time pitching a sales deal to Wayne; and just like some of my customers, he wanted to hide when he saw me coming.

Marriage

Nagging is not good:

It is better to dwell in a corner of the housetop, than with a brawling (nagging) woman in a wide house.
PROVERBS 21:9

Women, when you see your husband looking up at the ceiling, you might want to do something different. If you do what you've always done, you'll get what you've always gotten. In the following chapters, you will begin to see our mistakes, and I pray it will encourage you to do something different.

Go to the ant, thou sluggard; consider her ways, and be wise.
PROVERBS 6:6

I couldn't do this married thing without help. It takes too much work and I wasn't accustomed to working very hard at anything. I didn't work hard to get him, so why would I need to work hard to keep him?

Little did I know that the saying "work smarter, not harder" would be effective in my marriage. I applied that principle everywhere else in my life, and I was very successful, but I didn't think it would help my marriage. Working smarter, not harder means having the resources and the knowledge of what you are doing, as well as having enough common sense to realize that you can't do it alone.

When I think about all of the jobs I've had over the years, I've only worked hard at one of them. I loved the job, but the workload was overwhelming, and I couldn't see the overwhelming task ever coming to an end—which was scary for me. I'm sure you can guess what I did. I quit! Yes, I quit that job, just like that.

This is how most marriages end in divorce; they quit. Most married couples love their spouses, but they can't see the overwhelming tasks that their spouses have put on them will ever come to an end. Like me, they ask, will I have to work this hard every day for the rest of my life?

A few months before I turned in my two weeks' notice, I met with my boss and informed him that my assigned workload was overwhelming and that I needed help. However, he didn't see the need, because I was getting the job done. My work was always finished on time; I met all deadlines, continued smiling, and gave great costumer service. Yes, I was getting the job done, but it was killing me physically, mentally, and spiritually.

Every day after my meeting with my boss, little by little, I began to move my personal items out of the office—and he didn't even notice. Maybe he didn't notice because he only came to my office when he wanted something, or maybe he didn't care. Every time he came to my office, I called him an idiot. If I wasn't trying to live a godly life, I would have called him some other names; believe me, I do know some, and they all described him. How could he not see I needed help? Everyone else could; why couldn't he?

Even though I got paid well and received large bonuses, I had no respect for him—none!

Zero! Does this sound like your marriage?

In a marriage, when people can't see that the negative things will ever come to an end, they begin to search for ways to quit.

Killing Me Softly

Have you already moved your personal items out, and your spouse is not aware of it? Some spouses have "checked out" of their marriage and they are just living together. It is hard work living with someone who has checked out, because one person is now doing all the work.

At my job, I physically moved my personal items out of my office. In most marriages, the move is mental. One of the marriage partners has checked out in their minds. That is not a good place to be, but a lot of married couples are there. When a person checks out in their mind, they can live with you, sleep with you, have sex, and even ride with you to church on Sunday mornings while they never say a word or make any effort to make things better.

I have had people tell me that they don't understand why they are having marriage problems when they rarely talk or disagree. If you're not talking and you agree with everything your spouse says, you are probably not being honest—and you will never have a happy marriage without honesty.

When you've reached the point of silence—or shutting down—and not wanting to deal with your spouse in a meaningful way, you're in big trouble. You could be headed for a place that no married couple should be. You know that your marriage is being killed softly when you have not debated with your spouse about anything; in fact, you have not had an interesting conversation about anything that is important to either of you. Come on, let's admit it. One or both of you have initiated the silence in an effort to protect yourself, or to control the conversation—or maybe you're just not interested in dealing with the real issue.

When there is healthy debate or even heated arguing in a marriage, both spouses are trying to have their voices heard and get their points across. Opinions are expressed, and both of you know where the other stands. With silence, no one knows where the other stands. There is simply guessing and assuming.

I believe that silence in marriage is easy to cure. Consider doing what I do: just start talking. Stop playing "The Blame Game" and begin to understand why you shut down.

The Blame Game has been going on since the beginning of creation. Adam and Eve broke God's command by eating the fruit of the Tree of the Knowledge of Good and Evil. When God confronted Adam, he blamed his wife, and when Eve was confronted, she blamed the serpent.

The Blame Game will have you going around in circles in your marriage. Blaming each other won't accomplish anything, and it's not a cure for the silent treatment. What you have to say is important to you, right?

My sisters often laugh at Wayne and I, saying they've never seen a married couple disagree as much as we do and love on each other right after the disagreement. I continue to tell them we are not disagreeing; we are just trying to get our opinions heard. Once that occurs, right or wrong, we can work on the solution.

When the disagreement is over, and no matter how heated, he is still my husband, and I'm still his wife—and we must do it God's way.

There is a way which seemeth right unto a man, but the end thereof are the ways of death.

PROVERB 14:12

Harsh Words

Let no corrupt communication proceed out of your mouth, but that which is good to the use of edifying, that it may minister grace unto the hearers.

EPHESIANS 4:29

Harsh words can cause a person to shut down and eventually kill a marriage. Harsh words might make your mate check out. More than anything, I want married couples to know that your spouse is not your enemy. So stop hurting them with harsh words that kill!

Harsh words from someone you love can make the strongest man feel like a ten-year old boy and a confident woman feel like a failure. My mother always told me that a kind word goes further than a harsh word in any discussion, including the heated ones.

"Sticks and stones may break my bones, but words will never hurt me." Remember that rhyme?

I'm sure by now you know it is a lie. Words are very powerful. Words can hurt or heal, build up or tear down, comfort or curse. Proverbs 18:21 says, *"Death and life are in the power of the tongue; and they that love it shall eat the fruit thereof."* Are you eating the fruit of harsh words?

I grew up on a farm. Watching my father plant seed, with the expectation of it producing a harvest, was interesting. I can remember my father making a decision to plow up acres of cucumbers that he had planted weeks before. However, the next day, he replanted them. I was thinking to myself, this man has lost his mind! However, I learned he had plowed up the field because the seeds he'd planted were bad. Dad had planted cucumbers for many years, so he knew what to look for. Why let a vine produce fruit that you know you won't be able to enjoy?

Many married couples plant seeds in their marriage that are tasteless or downright nasty. I'll admit, Wayne and I both planted some seeds of harsh words, and we didn't like the way it tasted.

Oftentimes, we are too quick to say the things that come into our mind without evaluating whether they are edifying or not. We are so used to protecting ourselves that we save up harsh words like ammunition. When we feel that we are losing the battle, we come out with guns blazing like a Marine in combat, and we don't stop until our spouse has surrendered.

When you are hurting your spouse, you are hurting yourself. Why would you want to be so negative?

I used to work with a young lady who told me her husband would never help her out around the house or do anything for their six-year old daughter, but he was always kind to other people and willing to help them. Without even meeting the man, I began to form my own opinion of him. Boy, was I wrong.

After spending one afternoon with the two of them, I told her she should be thankful that he was still there. In a time span of two hours, she pretty much told this man that he was useless. She commented in a negative way on everything he did. If it didn't come out in her words, her body language said it.

She was so blinded by what he didn't or couldn't do that she never even noticed what he did. She would say to me, "Girl, I'm just telling him like it is; I'm just being honest." But she wasn't just being honest, she was being *brutally* honest. There is a difference. Honesty is a powerful tool and, like most tools, it can be used for good or evil. It can be used to build your spouse up, or it can be used to tear your spouse down. While the tone of your words play a huge role in determining the difference, your motivation plays an even bigger role.

Here's a more personal example. I had always wanted to dye my hair a color other than brown or black, and one day, I got the nerve to do it. After consulting with my hairdresser, I decided to go auburn. She mixed the chemicals and proceeded to color my hair. She loved it! However, when I looked in the mirror, I thought I was going to have a heart attack! I thought to myself, I cannot go home like this. What is Wayne going to say?

Marriage

My stylist could tell that I didn't like the color, so she toned it down with a rinse—but it was still red. I was disappointed and hurt, and I worried that what Wayne had to say would make me feel even worse. So I decided to call him from the hairdresser and tell him what had happened and how I felt about it. I also warned him that I did not need to hear anything negative from him; I was already feeling bad enough.

When I got home, I was surprised. He smiled and said he'd always wanted to sleep with a red-headed woman. He could have taken that opportunity to criticize me, but he decided to edify and build me up instead.

Most marriages cannot survive the constant condemnation of a spouse. Criticism doesn't encourage anyone to change; it forces them to give up. The more you focus on the negative, the more negative their feelings will become toward you and your marriage. Pretty soon, the love that he or she once had for you will turn into resentment and regret. Once that happens, walking away from you, the home that the two of you have built, and even your kids will become easy. You might feel that you've been abandoned, but they will feel freedom from constant condemnation.

Something is Missing

It sounds like we are really in love when we say a person "completes us." I used to say that all the time, and I do understand why we say it. Having a special person in our life can make us feel complete. But feeling complete and *being* complete are two different things.

If Wayne completes me, that means I'm half a person. It's too much pressure on anyone to have to complete another person. We weren't created to complete each other. Wayne wasn't formed to complete me; he was formed to protect and provide for me. I wasn't made to complete him; I was made to help him.

In the beginning of our marriage, I put so much pressure on him. Something was missing within me, and I was seeking completeness from him. He tried his best to give it to me. Not only was he providing and protecting, he was trying to fill a void in me that could only be filled by God. So no matter what he did, it wasn't good enough.

Marriage

A lot of people get married thinking that they'll have that sense of completion after the wedding. But then, two or three months later, they realize they are feeling worse than ever, and they begin blaming their spouse.

On my wedding night, the weirdest thing happened to me. I went to sleep and had a dream—that night, I called it a "nightmare," but now I call it revelation and truth. In the dream, I was being told that the void I felt within me could not be filled by the man lying beside me. That was scary for me, because I had gotten married thinking that my search for peace was over.

Wayne woke me up and, being the man that he is, assured me that he could and would fill the void. He was wrong—and I was wrong for believing him. Neither one of us knew any better. Remember me telling you in the beginning of this book that we both were spiritually dead? That void is a void that only God can fill.

People and things cannot complete people. We must release our spouses from the role of being God in our lives. When we put people in the place of God, we do not give them any room for error. When they do make mistakes—and they will, because we all do—we begin to feel like we married the wrong person. We might make statements like this: "I didn't know he did this." "I didn't know she was like that" No, you didn't know—but God did.

Look at it like this: when putting a puzzle together, there are several pieces. Each piece is complete, no matter how big or small. When you put it in its proper place, that piece helps make the puzzle. When we get married, we should be two complete people who come together, to be one.

> *"He replied, Have you never read that He Who made them from the beginning made them male and female, And said, For this reason a man shall leave his father and mother and shall be united firmly (joined inseparably) to his wife, and the two shall become one flesh? So they are no longer two, but one flesh. What therefore God has joined together let not man put asunder (separate)."*
> MATTHEW 19:4-6, AMP

The Scripture plainly says the *two* became one, not that two halves came together and became one. Stop looking at yourself as a half person. If you have God in your life, you are complete. Then no matter what your mate does or doesn't do, you are still complete.

I Am an Individual

Before I formed you in the womb I knew you, and before you were born I consecrated you.

JEREMIAH 1:5

Jeremiah 1:5 does not change because we get married. We will all stand in front of God as individuals.

The first five years of our marriage, I spent a lot of time trying to get Wayne in tune with my ever-changing ball of emotions. I was trying to change him. But in trying to force him to change, I lost who I was.

A lot of times, we might lose whatever it was that our spouse loved about us most as we try to change them or try to change ourselves to please them. Most people will say that their spouse is the reason—he or she isn't "being themselves" anymore. People will say, if my spouse would just change, then I could be the person I was when we first met. What a cop-out! And yet, so many of us have fallen into believing it.

Sit back and ask yourself, "Where is the original me—the person God created?"

Did you begin to slip away when your spouse told you the first lie? Was it when they had an affair the first time, or when you spent all day in the kitchen cooking and he/she didn't even say thank you? No matter what your spouse does, please do not allow yourself to lose who you are. Because the person God created you to be is the person they need—not the person you have allowed yourself to become trying to protect yourself.

I've learned that the best way to protect me is to be the "me" that God created:

"God created [us] in His own image, male and female He created [us]."

GENESIS 1:27

We were called, we were named, and we were claimed, even before we were born.

Wayne and I are so different. My husband is a thinker and a planner. I'm not; I don't think about anything, so what do I plan? I used to see our differences as a curse, but now I know they are blessings.

While driving home to see my parents in South Carolina one day, God reminded me that my husband being a thinker and planner was for my benefit. Wayne knows every exit on Interstate 95. When I had to drive home to South Carolina alone for the first time, Wayne gave me a detailed plan. He told me which exits to stop at for gas, because he wanted to ensure that I would be in a safe area.

Can you believe I missed the first exit? As soon as I did, the phone rang, and it was him. He knew exactly how long it would have taken me to get to that exit. I informed him that I had accidentally passed it; he had suspected I might, so he called to let me know which safe exit was coming up next.

If this had taken place earlier in our marriage, it would have ruined my trip. I would have interpreted his phone call as an attempt to control me. I probably would have turned around and gone back home, and satan would have won by taking some valuable time away from me.

Whose Money Is It?

I grew up in a God-fearing home, where my father was the head of the household and everyone knew it. Being in a position to take care of his family was important to him. My mother worked because she chose to, not because she had to. I don't recall a time when my siblings and I were in need of anything.

I've learned so much from my parents. As for our finances, obeying my father in this area has given me the liberty to work or be a stay-at-home wife and mother at any time. My father sat down with Wayne and told him the same thing he'd told me and my brothers and sisters. He said we should never purchase anything based on my income. "If you can't afford it based on your income only," he said, "don't purchase it."

My father's advice was based on what he believed, and it helped us. When I work, I always contribute to our household as a helpmate. Over the years, no matter what we bought, it was based on one income. We had to wait, at

Marriage

times, before we could get the things we wanted; however, waiting kept us from getting over our heads in debt.

Still, for some reason, we were never able to save. It was as if we had holes in our pockets and we could not get ahead. Anytime we managed to save a few dollars, we had to repair something. I just could not understand why.

I went to church one Sunday, and the pastor told the congregation to read Haggai 1:6-7:

Ye have sown much, and bring in little; ye eat, but ye have not enough; ye drink, but ye are not filled with drink; ye clothe you, but there is none warm; and he that earneth wages to put it into a bag with holes. Thus said the Lord of Host; consider your ways.

If you are in financial bondage, like we were, you might want to consider your ways. I've talked to a lot of women who work hard and take every opportunity to remind their husbands of their work, but their spending is out of control. They make comments such as, "I spend what I want, because it is my money." I don't know how many times I told Wayne this. What I really wanted to tell him was, "Why not spend it? You (Mr. Head of the House) don't have a financial plan for our family."

Whose Money Is It?

One day, while having a heated argument about our finances, I just blurted it out. His feelings were hurt, but he knew I was right; we didn't have a plan. I can remember him coming to me two days later and admitting we had to do something different. He said he had a plan.

And the LORD answered me, and said, Write the vision, and make [it] plain upon tables, that he may run that readeth it.

HABAKKUK 2:2

He had a financial vision for our family. It wasn't until I joined Wayne in his financial vision for our family that I began to see that he cared for the things most wives think their husband's don't notice. In his plan, I could work or choose not to. If I worked, my check would go into our savings account. He would pay the bills. We would both be given a weekly allowance, and we wouldn't buy anything that cost more than fifty dollars without talking to the other.

This was hard for me, because I believed I deserved to spend my own money. I wasn't a child! However, after some time, I started to go along with the plan. I began to see Wayne in a way that I had never seen him before.

Because he was in charge of the finances, he knew when to remind me of my hair and nail appointments. I no longer had to hide the new shoes and clothing I brought into the home, because he had given me the money to buy them. I wish we had worked this out early in our marriage. Now, we are on one accord with our finances, and he is more in tune with my personal needs. I no longer worry about our finances. I know Wayne will do the right thing.

God will supply all the things we need if we are obedient to His Word:

But my God shall supply all your need according to His riches in glory by Christ Jesus.

PHILIPPIANS 4:19

When it comes to finances, being of one accord with a God-given vision for your family is the key. Money is currency, and just like a current in the ocean, money comes and it goes. But you don't have to ever be in need, if you do things God's way.

If you haven't already, sit down with your spouse and discuss your finances. Come up with a plan. When the two of you agree on a plan, you can work together to accomplish it.

Can two walk together, except they be agreed?
                                                              AMOS 3:3

We made tithing and giving an offering a priority in our plan. A lot of people don't believe in tithing, but we do; tithing changed our lives. I can remember hearing the message on tithing for the first time. I was very skeptical, and Wayne turned a completely deaf ear to it.

Then, when I was sitting in worship service one Sunday, the Spirit of the Lord spoke to my heart, and told me to tithe. I went back and forth with the Lord, trying to convince Him, of all people, that I couldn't afford to tithe. "Lord I don't have any money," I said to Him over and over again. "I only have the money to put gas in my car so I can get to work."

I watched the offering plate as it was passed from person to person. I felt like I was going to pass out. But when it got to me, I put in all the money I had. I cried out to the Lord as Jacob did in Genesis 28:20-22 and said, "Lord you got to be with me, because I'm going to run out of gas!"

Marriage

Jacob vowed a vow, saying, If God will be with me, and will keep me in this way that I go, and will give me bread to eat, and raiment to put on,[21] *So that I come again to my father's house in peace; then shall the LORD be my God:*[22] *And this stone, which I have set [for] a pillar, shall be God's house: and of all that thou shalt give me I will surely give the tenth unto thee.*

GENESIS 28:20-22

Out of faith and faith only, I tithed the "gas money." From that time until now, I have never had to worry about gas for my car. God increased our finances and opened the windows of heaven over our lives, just like he said he would.

Bring ye all the tithes into the storehouse, that there may be meat in mine house, and prove me now herewith, saith the LORD of hosts, if I will not open you the windows of heaven, and pour you out a blessing, that [there shall] not [be room] enough [to receive it].

MALACHI 3:10

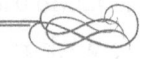

Whose Money Is It?

There is a saying, "You can't out-give God." Well, we found that to be true. When we included giving an offering to our financial plan, our lifestyle and our relationships with others changed. The more we gave, the more people gave to us. People that we didn't even know began to sow into our lives.

Give, and it shall be given unto you; good measure, pressed down, and shaken together, and running over, shall men give into your bosom. For with the same measure that ye mete withal it shall be measured to you again.

LUKE 6:38

So whose money is it? Wayne and I can truly answer that question by saying our money belongs to the Lord.

The earth [is] the LORD'S, and the fullness thereof; the world, and they that dwell therein.

PSALMS 24:1 (A PSALM OF DAVID)

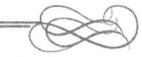

Why Do I Seem to Love Him More?

I've learned that, as much as Wayne loves me, my requirements and response to love are different from his. This made me wonder why it seems I love him more. I found the answer in Genesis 3:16-19. Because of Adam and Eve's disobedience to God, this is what God said to Eve:

Unto the woman He said, I will greatly multiply thy sorrow and thy conception; in sorrow thou shalt bring forth children; and thy desire shall be to thy husband, and he shall rule over thee.

GENESIS 3:16

Take a look at the meaning of the word "desire:"

To wish or long for.
To express a wish for.
To request or petition.

It's not that I love him more, we just express love differently. Based on the definition of desire, I do long for him, I express it daily, and like most women, I don't have a problem letting my request and petitions be known to him.

That's sound pretty good right? However, in this text, the word "desire" in its original "Hebrew" language means to control. God told Eve that she would try to control Adam, and this was my problem. I spent a lot of time trying to control the way Wayne expressed his love to me, so naturally, it would seem as if I loved him more.

This is what God said to Adam:

And unto Adam He said, Because thou hast hearkened unto the voice of thy wife, and hast eaten of the tree, of which I commanded thee, saying, Thou shalt not eat of it: cursed [is] the ground for thy sake; in sorrow shalt thou eat [of] it all the days of thy life; Thorns also and thistles shall it bring forth to thee; and thou shalt eat the herb of the field; In the sweat of thy face shalt thou eat bread, till thou return unto the ground; for out of

Why Do I Seem to Love Him More?

it was thou taken: for dust thou [art], and unto dust shalt thou return.

GENESIS 3:17-19

There are times that we may not be on our husbands' mind the way we would like. That doesn't mean they love us any less. They could simply be dealing with the "thorns and thistles" of life.

I can remember saying to Wayne, "Baby, I think about you all the time." It really hurt my feelings when he said to me, "Sweetie, I don't think about you all the time. I have other things on my mind." I asked, with a loud voice, "What things?"

I didn't realize that I am often on his mind. When he gets up for work, day after day, to provide for us, that shows me that I am on his mind. When he makes sure the lights are on and the bills are paid on time, I'm on his mind. When he gets up in the morning after a snow storm and cleans the snow off my car, I'm on his mind. When he calls the airline to check on the status of my fight and picks up my tickets in advance, I'm on his mind.

Please take the time to learn your spouse's love language. I'm sure he or she speaks love to you throughout the day, but if you don't recognize the language, you may not notice. Dr. Gary Chapman identified five love languages: Words of Affirmation, Quality Time, Receiving Gifts, Acts of Service, and Physical Touch. Wayne's love language is Acts of Service; mine is Words of Affirmation.

It took us some time, but once we found out how we both express our love, there was no way we could doubt our love for each other. As much as I would enjoy hearing Wayne say good things about me (Words of Affirmation), all day and every day, it drives him crazy when I say them to him. I've learned to cut back to one or two times. Then he says, "Okay, wash the dishes or sweep the floor! Then I'll know how much you appreciate me."

No Ordinary Love

There are four types of love:

- *Eros* love—known as "erotic love" is based on strong, romantic feelings towards another person.

- *Philos* love—a love based on friendship between two people who share a mutual, "give-and-take" relationship.

- *Storge* love—a physical show of affection that results from a pure motive. It includes fondness through familiarity, especially between family members or people who have otherwise found themselves together by chance.

- *Agape* love—unconditional love that is always giving and which makes it impossible to take or be a taker.

British singer Sade Adu sings a song called "No Ordinary Love." If you have never heard of the word *agape* before, please take the time and look it up. Agape isn't ordinary; it's not the type of love to which we're accustomed.

Agape is unconditional:

Love suffers long and is kind; love does not envy; love does not parade itself, is not puffed up; does not behave rudely, does not seek its own, is not provoked, thinks no evil; does not rejoice in iniquity, but rejoices in the truth; bears all things, believes all things, hopes all things, endures all things. Love never fails. But whether there are prophecies, they will fail; whether there are tongues, they will cease; whether there is knowledge, it will vanish away.

1 CORINTHIANS 13:4-8, NKJV

Agape love is a must in a marriage. Agape love is above philos, eros, and storge love. It is a love that is totally selfless, where a person gives out love to another person—even if this act does not benefit her/him in any way.

I believe all four types of love should be present in a marriage. I have romantic feelings toward Wayne; he is my best friend; and I have physical affection toward him. But it is the unconditional love that comes from God that holds our marriage together. Agape love loves when all other types of love are gone, and cares when there is no reason to care. The agape love of God goes past the surface, enabling me to look deep into Wayne's heart and love him for who God has made him, despite his faults. When all four types of love are in operation, the marriage is what God intended for it to be.

The Vows Make the Difference

And the rib, which the LORD God had taken from man, made He a woman, and brought her unto the man. And Adam said, This is now bone of my bones, and flesh of my flesh: she shall be called Woman, because she was taken out of Man.

GENESIS 2:22-23

God removed a *rib* from your man and formed you. Let's get background information on the rib. One of the Hebrew words for rib is "beam." God created woman to be a support beam to her husband.

The wedding vows are the heart of the wedding ceremony and the foundation for marriage. I've heard many people say that being married is not too much different than being engaged, dating, or living together. However, I feel like things are completely different; the vows make it different.

The first thing God taught me concerning wedding vows is that they shouldn't be taken lightly and there is power in the vows. It is better to not make a vow than to make it and not uphold it:

When thou shalt vow a vow unto the LORD thy God, thou shalt not slack to pay it: for the LORD thy God will surely require it of thee; and it would be sin in thee. But if thou shalt forbear to vow, it shall be no sin in thee.
DEUTERONOMY 23:21-22

When we vowed to be married, it became a covenant relationship between God, Wayne, and me. However, I had never heard of a covenant, so how in the world could I have a covenant marriage? After I found out more about covenants, it was no wonder we argued so much!

We looked at our marriage as a contract. We had *philos* love, a mutual "give and take." I had a list of things for Wayne to do, and when he didn't do them, I didn't respond as a loving wife. I'm one of those wives that must always respond, and there is nothing wrong with that. The problem was my mentality of "you rub my back and I'll rub yours." It sounds pretty good, but this is where I was going wrong.

The Vows Make the Difference

There were days Wayne came home after dealing with the thorns and thistles of the day and he didn't smile at me when he came in the door nor did he feel up to rubbing my back—but he did really need for me to be there for him. My naive thoughts condemned him for not coming into the house smiling, since I'm supposed to be the most important person to him. I had to learn to treat the marriage covenant with respect, no matter what.

It is my job as his wife to wrap myself around him in support—no matter what he gives me back, in that moment. In return, I've always been blessed.

Don't let a "contract mentality" keep you from being happily married. Whenever conditions and terms define a marriage, it is certain that the marriage will fail. Did you get married, or did you enter into a business deal? Only you and God know what is really in your heart.

You might say, "But he cheated on me!" Your marital vows make the difference, even if your spouse had an affair. Believe me when I say this: the other woman or man doesn't have as much power as you think. As a matter of fact, they are powerless when it comes to your marriage. How do I know? I experienced it.

When I learned that my husband had betrayed me, I was hurt, disappointed, ashamed, and angry. I was out of control! My emotions were in control. I'll never forget the day that it was revealed.

We were living in Jacksonville, North Carolina. Full of anger, I jumped in my car and drove to the state where

Marriage

this young woman lived. I can't remember the drive at all; I don't remember stopping at any stop signs or red lights, and I don't remember going over the bridge I was somewhat fearful of. I drove five hours. Wayne was in the car with me, but it was as if he wasn't there. I had already said what I needed to say to him. Now I wanted to talk to her.

When we arrived at her house, we both climbed out of the car. By this time, Wayne was in tears. He begged me not to enter the house, but I walked around him and went straight to the front door.

I found this to be strange, but the door was open, so I just walked in. I strolled through the house until I got to the back room, where an elderly lady was sitting. She gave me the biggest smile I've ever seen and said, "Hi, Sweetie! You are a pretty girl. What is your name?"

When she said those words to me, it seemed as if I awakened from a bad dream. I told her my name and then ran out of that house as fast as I could. Once I was back to my car, I felt completely alert.

Wayne looked at me and said, "I'm sorry. I don't want to lose my family." And I realized, at that moment, that I was thankful for my life. When you're thankful for life, the people who are most important come to mind—and Wayne was one of them. As devastated as I was, I still loved my husband.

I remembered the vows we had made to each other—and this other woman wasn't part of them. Her name was not included in our covenant marriage. Suddenly, I realized that she no longer mattered to me.

I say to every person who is having an affair, or maybe thinking about sleeping with someone else's spouse: "Don't do it." It only shows a lack of power.

If you are married, you can still have the power it takes to make your marriage work. It started on the day you vowed to be together until death. This is true whether you took those vows in the courthouse with a justice of the peace and a witness you had never seen, or whether you were in your local church with mom, dad, your twenty-four-person wedding party, and all the other people in the neighborhood you didn't invite. Your ability to be happily married started the day you said "I do," and no one else has the power to take that away from you:

Therefore what God has joined together, let no man put asunder (separate).

MATTHEW 19:6, AMP

If you don't believe me, take a few moments and talk to God. He will tell you that I am right. Your spouse is the only person God has given insight on how to take care of all of your needs. Yes, all of them! God has the answers to all the questions you have concerning your marriage. On your wedding day, when you made a promise to Him, He also made one to you.

Forgive Quickly

Forgive quickly. Be angry and sin not.

In a marriage, there are conflicts and challenges. How we deal with them will determine whether we remain married or throw in the towel. Early in our marriage, I could go from zero to one hundred in just a few seconds, but it would take me days, months, or years to get over anger. On the other hand, it takes a lot to get Wayne angry, and then he gets over it in no time.

Scripture tells us that a time will come when we will get angry. But it tells us not to *sin*. Getting angry is not a sin, but holding on to it is:

> *Be ye angry, and sin not: let not the sun go down upon your wrath.*
>
> EPHESIANS 4:26

That is why forgiveness is so important. Forgiveness is not an emotion, it is a decision. No one can make you forgive them; forgiveness is a choice that you make for your own peace of mind.

Holding on to anger and resentment can make your life miserable. Forgiveness is one of the ways we can love as God loves, because we decide to forgive someone, we are deciding to love him or her unconditionally.

Mother Teresa said, "If we really want to love, we must learn how to forgive." I know it's hard to be forgiving when you feel betrayed and disappointed, but remember, we all make mistakes.

Forgiving is not the same as forgetting; most of the time, you *won't* forget. If I had forgotten my disagreements with Wayne, I wouldn't be able to share this advice with you. When you forgive your mate, it does not mean that you allow them to continue hurting you, and it's not a sign of weakness—it's actually a sign of strength.

Our marriage grew stronger when we learned to forgive, letting go of those things which were behind us and focusing on the things that lie ahead:

Brethren, I count not myself to have apprehended: but this one thing I do, forgetting those things which are behind, and reaching forth unto those things which are before, I press toward the mark for the prize of the high calling of God in Christ Jesus.

PHILIPPIANS 3:13-14

We have years ahead of us, and we both want to see our dreams fulfilled. The past is over; neither one of us could go back and change it. God healed us from our past hurt and restored our marriage.

The healing process started when I was no longer being controlled by anger. The elderly lady that I encountered in that home spoke to the strength inside of me that I had been questioning. Those few words she said reminded me of who I was. I had been comparing myself to the other woman—a woman that I didn't even know.

When my anger was no longer in control, I was able to listen to what Wayne was saying. He asked me to forgive him, and I heard him clearly. He took full responsibility for what had happened. He didn't blame me or the other woman. Trust had been broken, but we spent time doing whatever it took to build it again. I reminded myself of what a good man he is and how he has always taken care of me and our boys. He spent as much time with me as he possibly could, and he was honest.

"No man has a good enough memory to make a successful liar."

–ABRAHAM LINCOLN.

More than anything, honesty was what I needed. Honesty is the key ingredient to trust, and marriages need trust to survive. When you discover that the person you love is dishonest, it cuts deep, and that kind of pain can damage a relationship.

Being honest with your spouse takes a little bit of effort; it's often easier to tell a lie. Unfortunately, the short-term benefits of a lie can have long-term consequences. When a lie is revealed, trust is undermined, and the feeling of security can be destroyed.

When you choose to let truth rule in your marriage, you will soon realize that you have nothing to hide, and honesty becomes an easier path. If you're going to be honest with your spouse, you got to be honest with *yourself*.

Forgive Quickly

Wayne had fallen prey to an adulterous affair he had not seen coming. He was blindsided, and—before he knew it—he was involved with a person he really did not know, although he was deceived into thinking he knew her well. God gives us every opportunity to walk away from temptation, but many of us choose to walk toward it.

Submit yourselves, then, to God. Resist the devil, and he will flee from you.

JAMES 4:7 (NIV)

There hath no temptation taken you but such as is common to man: but God is faithful, who will not suffer you to be tempted above that ye are able; but will with the temptation also make a way to escape, that ye may be able to bear it.

1 CORINTHIANS 10:13 (KJV)

Your Spouse Must Be First

Some may not realize it, but your spouse comes first in your life—right after God. This means you have to accept your husband or wife entirely, just as they are. There are things that God put in place in each of us, and no matter what, we cannot change them. The sooner we accept that, the easier life will be.

When we put our spouses before anyone or anything else on Earth, we will be rewarded. If you treat your husband like a king, he will treat you like a queen. The reason we don't treat our spouses like royalty is because we are afraid of being stepped on and not getting our own needs met. But have you ever seen a queen in need? I haven't.

But what if you are treating your mate like a king or queen, and in return, they treat you like a maid or servant. That means your husband doesn't know that he is a King, or your wife doesn't know that she is a Queen. Kings and queens require certain respect, and they know how to treat other royalty. The position demands it.

You and your best friend may have been together as long as you can remember, but it is your job to let that person know that your spouse is now your best friend and will always come first. Yes, I can go shopping—but after I make sure Wayne is taken care of and doesn't have any plans for the two of us. My marriage always takes priority over all other relationships.

I can't take my husband for granted. Wayne is the person I wake up to and fall asleep with. My friends and my family don't have to deal with my moods, or put up with my attitude–and they certainly don't put food on my table. My husband does all of those things, through God.

Wayne was a United States Marine, and he had a lot of things to deal with for many years. There were times when he had to be gone for months at time, and he was given no assurance that he would ever return. However, his position in our home didn't change. Every decision I had to make without him, I made with him in mind.

Once, when Wayne was in Iraq, I had to decide whether to move once again without him. I made the decision based on the things he and I had planned for our future. When the movers came and moved all of our items to the new home, I was excited—until I remembered that this was the third time I'd had to relocate without him! It was the third time I'd had to get a home clean and ready for a military housing inspection; the third time I'd had to open boxes and hang pictures and turn another house into a home; and the third time I'd had to do this while still running around taking our boys to all of their activities.

I thought: *This is too much for me.* I allowed negative thoughts to cloud my mind and it ruined the excitement of moving to a new home. All I could see was boxes on top of boxes that needed unpacking. I didn't know where to start. Even though I'd done this twice before, I was in tears.

Then the phone rang. It was Wayne. He always knew when to call! He said he was so glad to hear my voice and to know that the boys and I were well. His phone call put things back into perspective for me. He told me to just be grateful that I was in a home and safe, because at that moment, he was in the streets of Iraq, trying to stay alive so he could return home to us.

This is how a king treats his queen. No matter what is going on in his life, his reason for doing what he does is to protect his kingdom and find his way safely home.

I got up off the floor, pulled myself together, and called my sister to ask if she would come and help me get unpacked.

Respect Always

If your mate feels that you have no respect for them, they are going to feel unloved. No matter how much you say you love them, your disrespectful actions will speak louder.

I can truly say I have always respected my husband, but my actions were disrespectful at times. I simply didn't know any better. It was hard for him to point these actions out to me without making me defensive.

I did a year-long study with a group of married couples at my local church and in my community. In the group, when we sat and listened to our spouses, many of us were surprised to learn of ways we made them feel disrespected. Here are some of the ways husbands said their wives disrespected them:

Marriage

- Didn't listen to him
- Lied to him
- Interrupted him when he was talking
- Underestimated him
- Didn't take him seriously
- Made decisions without his input
- Didn't try to understand him
- Refused to accept his way of doing things; went behind him to do things over
- Made promises to others without consulting him
- Put down his family members
- Contradicted what he had told the children.

These are the things the wives said their husbands did that made them feel disrespected:

- Wanted to have sex even though they hadn't spent any time with her

- Didn't compliment her appearance, but did compliment other women

- Compared her cooking to his mother's

- Came home from work and didn't greet or acknowledge her

- Spoke harshly to her around others

- Left the house without saying where they were going

- Lied to her

- Didn't listen to her

- Didn't pray with her

- Contradicted what she had told the children.

If you are doing more than one of these things, I believe it's possible your spouse may feel as though you do not respect them. Remember, both men and women need respect.

How you treat your spouse's things, and even the gifts they give to you, also reflects how much you respect them. I learned a lesson about this from my sister and her husband. My brother-in-law had given my sister a pair of nice, silk pajamas one year. When we were staying overnight with family, somehow our sleepwear got mixed up. I ended up coming downstairs wearing the top of the silk pajamas and my younger sister was wearing the bottoms. We thought it was funny, but my brother-in-law got upset, because that was a gift that he had given his wife.

Be mindful of allowing your friends and family to borrow items that your spouse bought for you. My bother-in-law felt like my sister didn't respect the fact that he had taken the time to purchase such a nice gift for her. Once he expressed his feelings, we apologized for the mistake, and he knew again that he was respected.

Don't Forget the Sex

Let the husband render unto the wife due benevolence: and likewise also the wife unto the husband. The wife hath not power of her own body, but the husband: and likewise also the husband hath not power of his own body, but the wife.

1 CORINTHIANS 7:3-4

I love Wayne, and there are times that, no matter how close I am to him, it isn't close enough. I feel both loved and protected when I'm near him. Sex is a way for married couples to enjoy this kind of closeness.

It should be every married couple's desire to satisfy each other sexually. Both of you should be working, from day one of your marriage, on how to satisfy each other's needs, and your sexual relationship should improve over the years. Sex should be like a melody in a song. If you feel the rhythm and learn the rhythm, the melody will get better in time. Before you know it, the two of you have created a beat that moves from your heart to your feet.

I am a firm believer that, if you're not enjoying sex, it is your responsibility to change that. Many women are embarrassed to talk about sex, and many men really don't know how to talk about having great sex. If a man feels he isn't satisfying you sexually, his ego might get in the way, and he might not want to talk about it. That's why some women lie and say they are enjoying it, even when they are not.

Is your sex life less satisfying than you wish? Be sure your body is healthy. There may be some medical reason. Find out by contacting your family doctor, and then seek the face of God for healing.

If you are medically healthy but still not enjoying sex, it is your responsibility to find out why. As a married couple, you should learn what your spouse enjoys and what they don't, and you should teach your spouse what you enjoy and what you don't. You have to find the courage to tell each other what to touch, what not to touch, and how to touch what they are touching.

Wayne and I dealt with this early on in our marriage. It was our desire to make sure we both were enjoying sex. No matter when we are together sexually, my concern is pleasing him and his concern is pleasing me. Because that is our priority, we are able to figure out ways to make it work.

Intimacy is so important. Great sex starts before intercourse. The two of you should look at every interaction as an opportunity to nurture the flame that burns in the other's soul. Example: When you are talking to your spouse, speak to them in a way that will nurture the flame of passion. Look at them with an expression that lets them know you have passion for them. When you introduce your spouse to a group or an individual, do it in a way that shows that you share a passionate connection.

If you keep that flame burning continually, the sex act will come naturally—even if you have a headache.

God never intended for us to struggle with sex. If you are struggling, you need to go to the enemy's camp (Satan) and take back your desire to have sex. If you have a headache, read a Scripture on healing.

If you have been lying to your spouse, saying you enjoy sex when you really do not, start being honest now. If you lie in this area, it opens the door for you to lie in other areas of your relationship. Scripture says,

> *"Defraud ye not one the other, except it be with consent for a time, that ye may give yourselves to fasting and prayer; and come together again, that satan tempt you not for your incontinency."*
>
> 1 CORINTHIANS 7:5

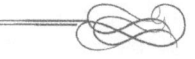

Yes, there will be times we just don't feel like having sex, but it shouldn't be every night—or should I say, every *day*, since sex isn't limited to night.

Always keep your bedroom special. Make it the most special room in your house. Teach your children to respect the privacy of your bedroom, from a very young age, so they understand that when the door is shut, you and your spouse are spending special time with each other that is not to be violated.

Wayne and I didn't teach our boys this—they taught us. Our boys, from a very young age, never wanted to come into our bedroom. It wasn't until they were older that they told us why. Our oldest son said he felt that he didn't belong in our bedroom because it was our special place. He knew if he needed something, he was welcome—but then he got what he needed and got out as quickly as possible.

Prayer Changes Things

Pray for your spouse. Pray for your marriage. I grew up in a family that prayed, and I know that I'm where I am today because the Lord answered the prayers of my mother and father.

Prayer makes a difference. It "works."

I pray because I know Wayne and I are in a battle. The Scripture warns of the devil's intention to demoralize us.

> *"Our struggle is not against flesh and blood, but against the rulers, against the authorities, against the powers of this dark world and against the spiritual forces of evil in the heavenly realms."*
>
> EPH. 6:10

Marriage

When we are in a battle, we need the help of God.

When we pray, God not only listens, but He speaks and answers our requests according to His will. His will is his "Word." When it comes to prayer, I always think about Hezekiah and how God added years to his life because he prayed.

In those days was Hezekiah sick unto death. And the prophet Isaiah the son of Amoz came to him, and said unto him, Thus saith the LORD, Set thine house in order; for thou shalt die, and not live. Then he turned his face to the wall, and prayed unto the LORD, saying, I beseech thee, O LORD, remember now how I have walked before thee in truth and with a perfect heart, and have done that which is good in thy sight. And Hezekiah wept sore. And it came to pass, afore Isaiah was gone out into the middle court, that the word of the LORD came to him, saying, Turn again, and tell Hezekiah the captain of my people, Thus saith the LORD, the God of David thy father, I have heard thy prayer, I have seen thy tears: behold, I will heal thee: on the third day thou shalt go up unto the house of the LORD. And I will add unto thy days fifteen years; and I will deliver thee and this city out of the hand of the king of Assyria; and I will defend this city for mine own sake, and for my servant David's sake. And Isaiah said, Take a lump

of figs. And they took and laid it on the boil, and he recovered. And Hezekiah said unto Isaiah, What shall be the sign that the LORD will heal me, and that I shall go up into the house of the LORD the third day? And Isaiah said, This sign shalt thou have of the LORD, that the LORD will do the thing that he hath spoken:

2 KING 20:1-9

The Lord has entrusted many things to Wayne and I, and we must pray to be good stewards over the things He has given us. He has given us each other.

Wives, pray for your husband's leadership in your marriage. Ask God to give him strength to carry out his responsibilities. Husbands, pray for your wife's role. Ask God to give her strength to carry out her responsibilities as your helper.

In prayer, God holds a mirror up to our lives so we can see the way we really are. Not only does prayer change things—it changes people. You may not agree with everything your spouse is doing. If you want things to change, take it to the Lord in prayer.

Notes

As you pray use the following pages to write your thoughts, plans and concerns for your marriage. Before you realize it, you will have begun your own manuscript. A manuscript you may one-day share with a group, a friend or the world. The goal is to write with the intent to move in the direction God would have you to move towards in your marriage. You will notice the words you write will begin to reflect God's Word, and the love He has for you and your husband.

_____
_____
_____
_____
_____
_____
_____
_____
_____
_____

Marriage

Notes

Marriage

Final Thoughts

In closing, I wrote this book with this Scripture in mind:

How shall we escape, if we neglect so great salvation; which at the first began to be spoken by the Lord, and was confirmed unto us by them that heard Him.

HEBREWS 2:3

Our salvation gives us the ability to pray to the Father in the name of Jesus, believing God will help us.

Some people see salvation as only a "fire protection plan" from hell. Salvation is much more than that. We may not go to hell, because of our salvation, but we can live in hell right here on earth when we don't receive all that our salvation offers. If you don't believe me, talk to someone who is in a bad marriage.

Marriage

If you have accepted Jesus and you are on your way to Divorce Court, it's because you—as a married couple—did not do it God's way! There is always time to change yourself and start again. Remember, God has given us everything we need to succeed, in marriage and in every area of our life.

Lavetta Wilson McClam

A Prayer for You

Thanks for letting me share my life with you. However, there is a man who gave His life for you. That man is Jesus Christ. You may have been married more than fifty years, or newly married, or you may not be married at all. If you have never accepted the man who gave up His life for you, now is a good time to do so.

Repeat these words and believe them. Then, just as He (Jesus) saved my life and my marriage, He will do the same for you:

> *Lord, I come to you, recognizing that I am a sinner and I have not lived a life that is pleasing to you. I believe that You died on the cross, taking my sins upon You. I believe that You were raised from the dead and You now*

live. Jesus, I accept You into my heart. I accept You as my Lord and Savior.

I know that I am saved now.

In Jesus' Name, Amen.

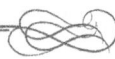

About the Author

Author and motivational speaker Lavetta Wilson McClam, is available for book signings, workshops, seminars, retreats, or other speaking opportunities. She can be reached at: mcclam221@gmail.com

Marriage: God Created it, I'm Loving It focuses on a married couple that you, the reader, can relate to. The author is transparent as she shares her thoughts and their experiences. Topics covered include Harsh Words, Whose Money is it?, No Ordinary Love, The Vows Make the Difference, Forgive Quickly, and Prayer Changes Things.

Marriage: God Created it, I'm Loving It was written, to give hope in a time when people are giving up on marriages. After reading it, you will have faith, hope, love, and a renewed spirit concerning your marriage. You will see that what you may be experiencing in your marriage is not unique.

Lavetta Wilson McClam is a native of Lake City, South Carolina. She believes in living life to the fullest. She holds a Business Management Degree and has been given the opportunity to organize and speak at events around the world.

Lavetta is an advocate for marriages who loves being married. She has been married to Retired Master Sergeant Wayne B. McClam for twenty-five years. Lavetta see every opportunity as a chance to share the goodness of God.

For years, Lavetta has been facilitating group meetings with married couples, encouraging them to remain faithful to their vows. She gives God all the Glory and Praise for giving her the opportunity to share her passion with others.

www.ingramcontent.com/pod-product-compliance
Lightning Source LLC
Chambersburg PA
CBHW032017040426
42448CB00006B/649